This book belongs to

Princess

 # Spot 10 differences

 # Tracing worksheet

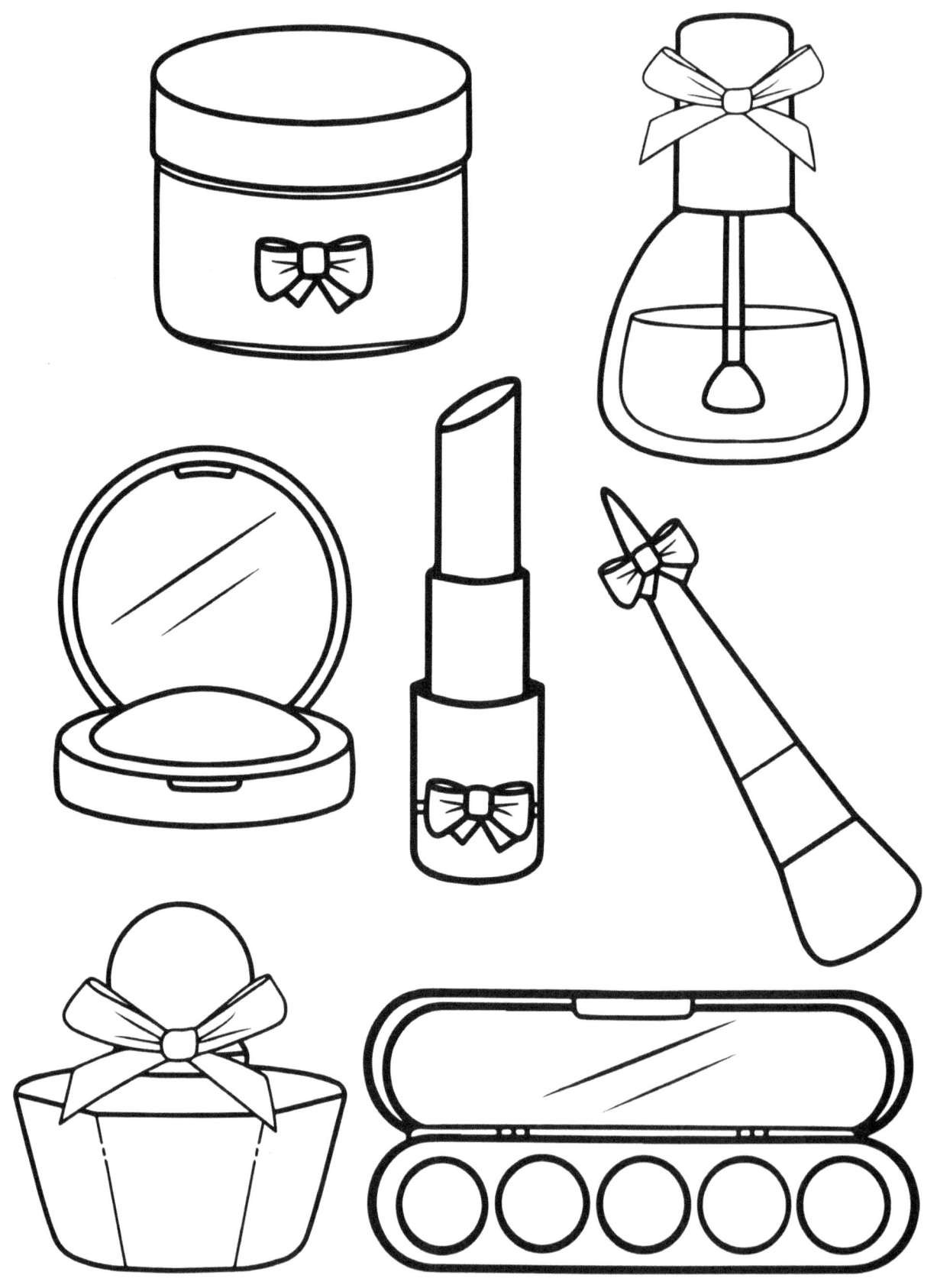

Draw a beautiful princess.

princess

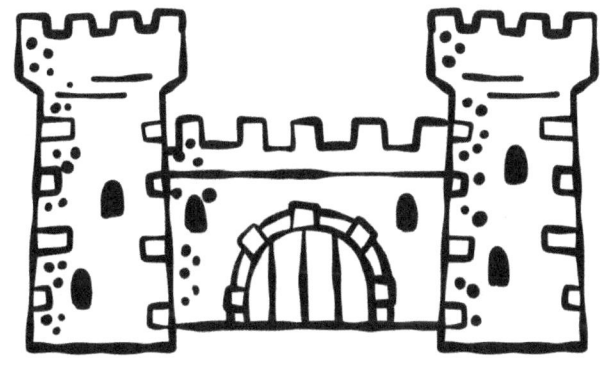

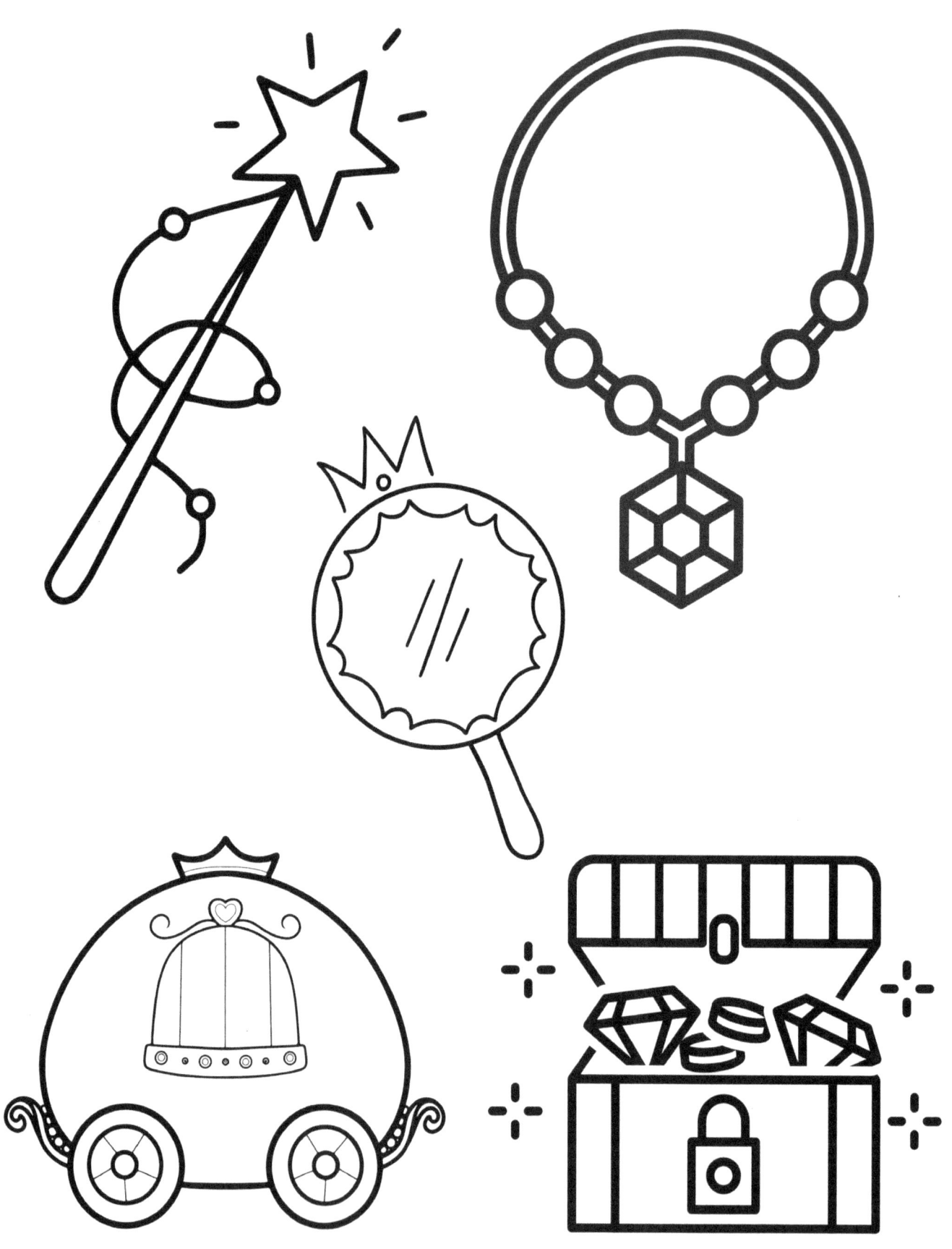

 What comes next?

LITTLE PRINCESS

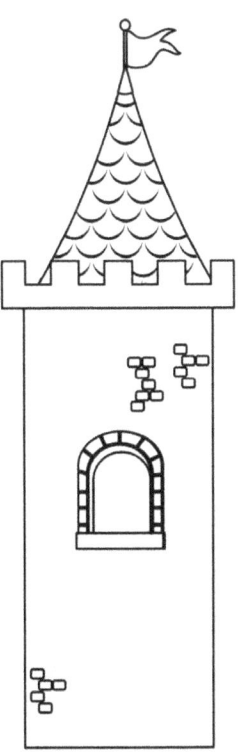

_____

_____

_____

_____

_____

_____

_____

_____

_____

_____

_____

_____

Draw a handsome prince.

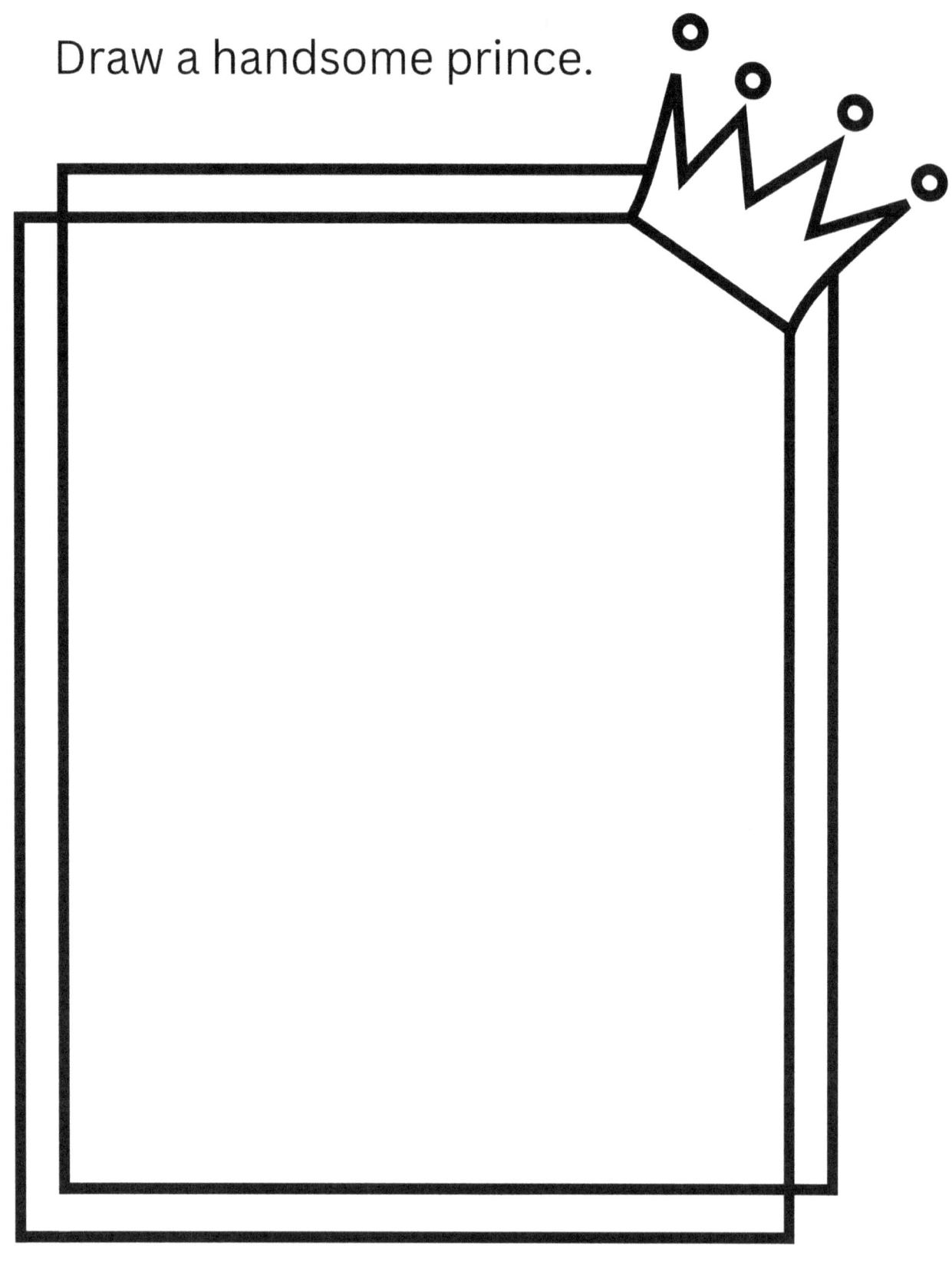

www.ingramcontent.com/pod-product-compliance
Lightning Source LLC
LaVergne TN
LVHW081540060526
838200LV00048B/2154